James

TERRIBLE CLAW
the story of a carnivorous dinosaur

Rwan

BEVERLY HALSTEAD D.Sc.
(Reader in Geology and Zoology, Reading University)

pictures by
JENNY HALSTEAD

COLLINS

William Collins Sons & Co Ltd
London · Glasgow · Sydney · Auckland
Toronto · Johannesburg

First published 1983
© text Beverly Halstead 1983
© illustrations Jenny Halstead 1983
ISBN 0 00 104112 6
Printed in Hong Kong by South China Printing Co.

For Thomas

Introduction

It was not until 1969 when Professor John Ostrom of Yale University described *Deinonychus antirrhopus* (the name means 'terrible claw'), that the fiercest flesh-eating dinosaur of all was first known. It had been found in rocks of the Lower Cretaceous period, formed about 120 million years ago, and came from the Cloverly Formation in Montana, U.S.A.

Deinonychus was two metres high and three metres long. It walked on its hind legs, and its most interesting feature was an enormous sickle-like claw on each hind foot. When *Deinonychus* walked or ran this claw could be raised out of the way. There were three sharp claws at the end of its long fingers for grasping and tearing, and the hand could rotate on the wrist; something no other known dinosaur could do. The long tail was completely rigid, able only to move up and down, and acted as a balancing pole.

There is evidence that deinonychosaurs hunted in packs and were capable of tackling animals much larger than themselves. This story is about the sort of life one *Deinonychus antirrhopus* might have lived. She is a female and we have called her Rhopa.

High on a rocky hillside overlooking a great plain, a mother
Deinonychus had buried her clutch of 16 eggs. Now faint tapping
and high pitched squeaks could just be heard. The mother
scraped away the sand with her long fingers, the eggs cracked and
the babies broke free. The mother picked them up gently, some
in her mouth and some in her long fingers. She carried nine of
them into the safety of the undergrowth where she had scraped
out a new nest. But as she returned for the remainder, two large
lizards fled between the rocks leaving dead and halfeaten
hatchlings among the broken eggshells. The mother moved
quickly back to her new nest. She scratched at the ground and
insects flew into the air: grasshoppers, beetles and termites were
eagerly snapped up by the babies with their small sharp teeth.
Wherever she went she was followed by her young, and the first
to follow was Rhopa.

Crocodiles, relatives of the flesh-eating dinosaurs, look after their hatchlings. In 1979 dinosaur nurseries were discovered, proving that advanced dinosaurs also cared for their young.

At night-time, as the air began to cool, the babies slowed down and their mother led them back to their nest. In the mornings they woke intertwined, and slowly began to wriggle. It was not until the sun was quite hot that they were ready to forage. One morning, when the young ones were a few weeks old, their mother had left them to go hunting. As they lay sleeping on each other, a hungry male *Deinonychus* discovered the nest. Plunging his three-fingered hands into the nest, he snatched three of the babies up into the air. They all struggled desperately, squeaking as loudly as they could. He carried two of them off to be eaten, dropping one in his haste. Rhopa and the other babies ran frantically in all directions. The mother heard the commotion and hurried back to find only six of her offspring still alive.

This episode is based on the discovery in New Mexico in 1947 of numerous skeletons of the two-legged, lightly-built flesh-eater *Coelophysis* in which several skeletons had the remains of young individuals of the same species inside their stomachs.

After a few months had passed, the six young deinonychosaurs were about one metre long. Each morning they stretched out in the sunshine to warm their bodies. Soon they were full of energy for snapping up insects and also for hunting. One day, they noticed several large lizards, nearly twice as long as they were, also warming up on the rocks. The deinonychosaurs stayed close together, rushed over and pounced on one of the lizards. With their clawed hind feet and fingers they tore it apart, feasting on its remains.

The young deinonychosaurs were cold blooded and needed the sun's heat but, because they were smaller, they warmed up faster than the lizards and so were able to catch them. Some lightly-built flesh-eaters, *Compsognathus*, have lizard remains preserved in their stomachs.

When Rhopa and the other deinonychosaurs were a year old their tails began to stiffen and the large claw on the hind feet to harden. Their mother left them to rejoin her old pack. One morning they came across a group of young plant-eating *Protoceratops*. One of the deinonychosaurs leapt on the nearest *Protoceratops* sinking his claws into its neck. There was a tremendous struggle, but the *Deinonychus* could not free himself. Both dinosaurs were severely injured and died locked together. Suddenly the mother *Protoceratops* appeared. She lowered her huge head and charged the deinonychosaurs, who fled.

In 1971 in the Gobi Desert the complete skeletons of a young deinonychosaur and a *Protoceratops* were discovered locked in exactly the position shown in the illustration. The large bony frill of *Protoceratops* is believed to have been a display to frighten away enemies. Notice the rose and oak in the picture which flourished at this time.

The five brothers and sisters were now two years old and had reached their adult size. During the heat of the day they would often go into the shallow waters at the edge of the lakes. As Rhopa and the others played in the warm water, frogs would jump off the water-lily leaves and swim away. The dinosaurs liked chasing them and snapping them up in their jaws or catching them in their long fingers. Small turtles paddled through the water weeds.

In 1980 the first evidence came to light in Connecticut that the two-legged flesh-eating dinosaurs were able to swim. Fossil prints were found, made when the back claws just scraped the muds and sands on the bottom. Frogs as well as many familiar birds such as flamingoes, and early rails and waders lived at this time.

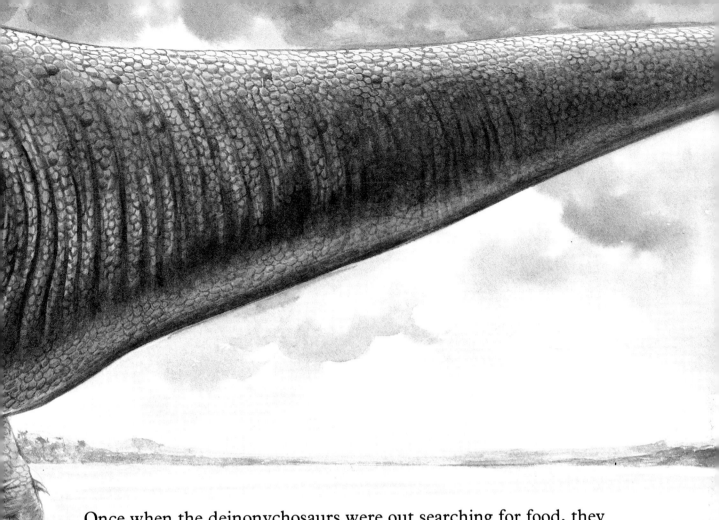

Once when the deinonychosaurs were out searching for food, they came across the huge flesh-eater *Tyrannosaurus* gorging itself on the remains of a corpse of a brontosaur. Rhopa hesitated but the smell of meat was overpowering and the five slowly edged forwards. *Tyrannosaurus* turned and bared its teeth and roared but did not move. The five *Deinonychus* dashed in, snatched pieces of meat and darted away.

The twelve-metre long ***Tyrannosaurus***, and other large flesh-eaters were slow moving and likely to have been primarily scavengers. The bones of a brontosaur's fleshy tail have been found with scratches which match the pattern of teeth of giant flesh-eaters. Broken teeth were found at the same spot. Brontosaurs survived over many millions of years to the end of the age of dinosaurs.

In the twilight, small furry mammals came out to feed. Some were plant-eaters, others searched for slugs, snails, worms and insects. And at the same time the deinonychosaurs came out to hunt the mammals. The evening hunts along the edge of the forests brought them into contact with another small pack of deinonychosaurs. Both groups joined forces so that they were now a pack of eleven, and a strong fierce male from the new group became the leader.

Deinonychosaurs had extremely large eyes which indicates that they could hunt in poor light. The small furry mammals included opossums, tree shrews and squirrel-like herbivores.

With eleven members the pack was tremendously successful at attacking and killing. They would run, gathering speed as they approached their victim, then would spring high into the air and with a violent kick of their sickle claws would rip open their prey. Even the brontosaur *Euhelopus* was quickly killed as it was ripped to shreds. The pack then dived in to feast; the new leader and Rhopa were always the first to eat their share.

> Skeletons of *Euhelopus* from China indicate that it was eleven metres long, compared to the three metres of the deinonychosaurs.

In the dry season the ground was baked hard, the plants were brittle from lack of water. One year there was a sound of fierce crackling, the wind was hot, the sky filled with smoke, blotting out the sun. Flames jumped from tree to tree as the roar of a forest fire spread. Dinosaurs, mammals, lizards, everything that could move, fled from the heat. The pack broke up in their fear, but Rhopa and the leader stayed together, running as fast as they could towards the safety of the waters of the lake.

Fossil charcoal has been found in rocks and proves the existence of ancient forest fires. The fires may have started from volcanic eruptions, but more probably, dry lightning ignited the plant material, and the flames were fanned by the wind. The undergrowth comprised shrubs and trees of ash, birch, holly, oak and dogwood.

After the fire had burnt itself out, the landscape was barren.
Rhopa and the leader had survived but their pack had vanished.
Many of the survivors waded in the shallows looking for food.
Herbivores like the duck-billed dinosaurs, managed on the weeds
in the lake, when they could not get their accustomed food of pine
needles and cones. For Rhopa and the leader there was no
problem: the weakened herbivores provided an abundant mass
of food, and they gorged themselves on a bonehead
dinosaur *Stegoceras*.

Slow-moving dinosaurs were doomed in a forest fire, whereas the lightly-built dinosaurs, such as *Deinonychus*, were capable of running ahead of the flames. Some water-loving dinosaurs, such as the brontosaurs, would have managed to survive. The diet of the duck-billed dinosaur is known from pine needles and pine cones found in the stomachs of their fossil forms.

With the coming of the rainy season new green growth quickly sprang up through the blackened landscape. Rhopa was now three years old and ready for mating. The leader approached her. He placed his forelimbs on her shoulders and twisted his body so that the underside of his tail could come in contact with Rhopa's and they mated.

Soon Rhopa moved up into the rocky outcrops in the hills, and there, with other females she found a secluded spot and scooped a hollow in the sand. She squatted down and began to lay her eggs. After each egg was laid she swivelled round so that they were laid in a circle, with a further circle on top of the first. She covered them with sand and for the next three months rarely left the nest site.

Dinosaur nesting colonies were discovered in Montana in 1982. The preservation of nests of dinosaur eggs in Mongolia and China shows that they were laid in neat rings, with a second row carefully positioned on top of the first.

Rhopa was always on the watch for other flesh-eaters, but she had to leave the nest once a day to search for food. Once, while she was away, four ostrich-dinosaurs moved in and uncovered several nests with their feet, breaking open the eggs with their beaks. On her return, Rhopa raced towards them but they turned and fled.

Rhopa covered her remaining eggs and in time six babies hatched out. Now Rhopa had to catch food which she regurgitated for them. She also had to keep a look out for snakes.

An ostrich-dinosaur, *Oviraptor* (the name means egg-catcher), was discovered in Mongolia on top of a nest of *Protoceratops* eggs which had been disturbed. The first snakes lived in burrows in the sand and would have eaten young dinosaurs. Birds feed their young by regurgitating their prey and this is likely to have been the case with the deinonychosaurs as it seems that modern birds are the direct descendants of lightly-built flesh-eating dinosaurs.

Across the plain on the edge of the marshy ground, in search of
food, Rhopa met another deinonychosaur pack, as they were
closing in on a large herbivore, a *Tenontosaurus*. Unfortunately
the ground was too soft for them to leap and as they attacked, the
thick, muscular tail lashed them and several fell stunned into the
mud. The *Tenontosaurus* was badly wounded and also fell to the
ground. As it rolled over, several deinonychosaurs were crushed
to death. Those that had their sickle claws embedded in the skin
were trapped and many had their legs broken. Rhopa managed
to break free but both her sickle claws were broken; she had lost
her main weapon for attacking her prey.

The first discovery of *Deinonychus* in Montana was of the remains of six individuals mixed up with those of a single large herbivore, *Tenontosaurus*. This association of one prey and six predators suggests that an episode similar to the one described almost certainly took place.

Bruised and wounded, she limped away, unable to keep up with the rest of the pack, but knowing she must escape before the already approaching scavengers arrived to devour what was left of the dead and wounded.

Although Rhopa could no longer deal with active prey, her killing instincts were just as keen and were increased by her pangs of hunger. She followed a small pack of deinonychosaurs through the rocks as they leapt after a herd of boneheads and she was able to survive on their leavings. Rhopa was no longer a hunter: she was a scavenger. On one occasion they came across the carcase of a deinonychosaur but they did not recognise it as one of their own kind; it was simply a welcome source of food and they all greedily feasted off it. Suddenly there was a sound of huge wings and, looking up, they saw the giant vulture-like scavenger, *Quetzelcoatlus*, who drove off the deinonychosaurs.

Reptiles, as well as hunting for their food, will devour any animal protein that comes their way: it is simply food. They make no distinction between their own and other species. In 1975 the fossil remains of the giant pterosaur *Quetzelcoatlus* were discovered in Texas and its wings were calculated to have been at least ten metres across.

Rhopa hid among the rocks until a slow moving ankylosaur, *Palaeoscincus*, passed. This seemed an easy prey and she hurled herself at it. With a quick movement the ankylosaur twisted itself sideways, and a row of sharp spikes was turned upwards. Rhopa landed directly on them with all her weight and was killed. The ankylosaur plodded on its way, leaving Rhopa lying among the rocks.